Science In Your Life:

SOUND
Listen Up!

Wendy Sadler

Raintree

© 2006 Raintree
Published by Raintree,
a division of Reed Elsevier, Inc.
Chicago, Illinois

Customer Service   888–454–2279

Visit our website at www.raintreelibrary.com

Printed by South China Printing Company

10 09 08 07 06
10 9 8 7 6 5 4 3 2 1

**Library of Congress Cataloging-in-
Publication Data**
Sadler, Wendy.
  Sound : listen up! / Wendy Sadler.
    p. cm. -- (Science in your life)
  Includes bibliographical references and index.
  ISBN 1-4109-1552-2 (library binding-hardcover) --
ISBN 1-4109-1560-3 (pbk.)
  1. Sound--Juvenile literature. I. Title.
  QC225.5.S23 2006
  534--dc22

                            2005014640

Acknowledgments
Alamy Images pp. 16 (Dynamic Graphics/ Photis),
15 (Lebrecht Music & Arts Photo Library), 10 (Robert
Harding Picture Library Ltd), 27 (PHOTOTAKE Inc.);
Corbis pp. 26 (Royalty Free), 4 (Gabe Palmer), 23 (Joe
McDonald), 11 (Ted Soqui); Getty Images pp. 6, 7, 9,
14, 22, 25 (PhotoDisc); Harcourt Education Ltd
pp. 8, 13, 17, 18, 20, 21t, 21m, 21b, 29 (Tudor
Photography); Imagestate p. 24 (Frank Chmura);
Photographers Direct p.5 (Transparencies, Inc.).

Cover photograph of sports coach blowing a whistle
reproduced with permission of Getty/Altrendo.

Every effort has been made to contact copyright
holders of any material reproduced in this book.
Any omissions will be rectified in subsequent
printings if notice is given to the publishers.

The paper used to print this book comes from
sustainable resources.

Disclaimer
All the Internet addresses (URLs) given in this book
were valid at the time of going to press. However,
due to the dynamic nature of the Internet, some
addresses may have changed, or sites may have
changed or ceased to exist since publication. While
the author and publishers regret any inconvenience
this may cause readers, no responsibility for any
such changes can be accepted by either the author
or the publishers.

An adult should supervise all of the activities in
this book.

Contents

Any words appearing in the text in bold, **like this**, are explained in the glossary.

Sound Is All Around You

Sound is all around you! When you close your eyes and listen hard, you can hear sounds you did not notice before. You can tell which sounds come from far away and which sounds come from nearby.

When you finish reading this page, close your eyes for a few seconds and listen hard. What can you hear?

You may have made some very loud sounds today!

Think about all the different sounds you have heard today. Where did they come from? How many of the following sounds have you heard?

- alarm clock beeping to wake you up
- people speaking to you
- music playing on the radio
- voices coming from the television
- eggs sizzling in the frying pan
- birds singing
- traffic moving through the streets.

How many things in this kitchen make a sound?

What Is Sound?

Sound is a very fast movement called a **vibration**. The vibrations move too quickly for us to see, but they can move through air, liquids, and even solid objects.

Sound travels through **materials** as a wave. If you throw a stone into a pond, you see ripples moving outward from where the stone hits the water. Sound waves travel in a similar way, but you cannot see them.

Sound waves are made when something vibrates. The waves spread out like ripples in a pond.

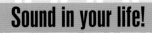

Sound in your life!

Next time there is a thunderstorm, try counting how many seconds there are between the lightning flash and the thunder crash. When there is a lot of time between them, the storm is far away. If there is not much time, then the storm is close.

Sound travels very quickly, around 1,115 feet (339.8 meters) in just 1 second! But this is a lot slower than light. Sometimes in a thunderstorm you see lightning first and then hear a crash of thunder later. The thunder and lightning actually happen at the same time, but the light reaches you before the sound does.

How Do We Make Sound?

Sound **vibrations** are very fast movements backward and forward, or side to side. We can make sound by making something vibrate.

When you pluck a guitar string, you pull it a little bit in one direction and then let go. The string moves from side to side very quickly. This vibration makes a sound. The wood of the guitar box also vibrates, and this helps make the sound louder.

A guitar is a string instrument. The strings vibrate to make the sound.

You can also make sound by hitting something. When you clap your hands, the air between them vibrates quickly. We hear this as a sudden sharp sound.

This is also the way that sound is made in a thunderstorm. When lightning strikes, the air around it gets hot very quickly. The air **expands,** and this starts a **shockwave** that makes the rumble of thunder.

Try to clap your hands as loud as you can. How much sound can you make?

Echoes

Sound waves can bounce off hard **surfaces** and travel back to where they came from. This is called an **echo**. In a big room or a large cave, there can be quite a long time between hearing the sound you make and then hearing the echo come back to you. This is because the sound has farther to travel, so it takes longer. This is why there are better echoes in large places.

A clap is a good sound to make echo within a cave.

If something **reflects** sound, the sound bounces off. If something **absorbs** sound, it takes the sound in. Hard, shiny surfaces are good at reflecting sounds and making echoes. Dull, soft surfaces are good at absorbing sounds. They do not make echoes.

In bathrooms there are usually lots of hard, shiny tiles on the wall. They reflect a lot of sound. This means that your voice sounds louder when you are singing in the shower!

Concert halls have lots of shiny surfaces to help reflect the sounds of the orchestra.

Sound in your life!

Try singing in a room that has curtains, carpets, and other soft things in it. What is the sound like? Now try singing in the bathroom. Does it sound different?

11

What Is Music?

To make music you need to put different sounds together in the right way. Music needs to have a mix of different **notes** so that it is interesting to listen to. High notes are sounds that have fast **vibrations**. They have a high **pitch**. Low notes are ones that have slow vibrations. They have a low pitch.

The **volume** of a sound is how loud it is. Music is made up of sounds that are different volumes. Loud sounds have lots of **energy**, and quiet sounds have less energy.

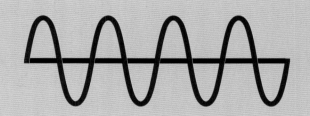
Fast vibrations = high pitch

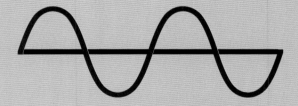
Slow vibrations = low pitch

When there are lots of waves close together, they make a high pitch. When the waves spread out, they make a low pitch.

Music also has something called **rhythm**. This means that long and short notes are put together to make patterns in the music. The rhythm is the part of the music that makes you want to dance or tap your feet.

Sound in your life!

Put your hand on your chest and feel your heartbeat. Your heartbeat has its own rhythm. When you are running around, it has a fast rhythm. When you are resting or sleeping, it has a slow rhythm.

13

Making Music

To make music, you need to make something **vibrate**. Different musical instruments make vibrations in different ways.

String instruments, such as guitars and violins, use the vibrations of the strings to make music. You play a violin using a bow made of lots of fine hairs. As the bow rubs across the strings, it sticks to the string, then slips away again very quickly. This sticking and slipping makes the strings vibrate.

A violin has strings that can be plucked with the fingers or played with a bow.

Wind instruments, such as recorders or flutes, use vibrating air to make sounds. **Percussion** instruments, such as drums or cymbals, have to be hit to make a sound.

A piano could be called a percussion instrument or a string instrument! Inside the piano are tiny hammers and a lot of strings. When you press a key, the hammer hits the string inside to make the sound.

strings

Inside a piano there are lots of small hammers that hit strings to make sounds.

Recording Sound

When you listen to music on a compact disc, or CD for short, you are hearing a recording of the singer or the group. When you make a recording, you use a microphone to turn the sound waves into electric waves. The electric waves can be saved and played back later when you want to enjoy the music.

You can carry recorded music with you wherever you go!

What would happen without CDs?

If we did not have music recordings or CDs we could only listen to music when it is played live. A music recording lets you listen to your favorite music any time and almost anywhere.

A CD
stores music
as a pattern
of numbers.

Most people now listen to music on CD or **MP3** players. This is called **digital** recording. To make a digital recording you have to turn the pattern of sound waves into numbers. Inside your CD player a **laser beam** reads these numbers as a **code**. The code is then turned back into a sound wave so you can enjoy your favorite tunes!

How Do We Hear?

We use our ears to hear sound. The flaps of skin on the sides of your head are shaped so that they can catch sounds as they come through the air.

Sound in your life!

Try making cup shapes with your hands and putting them around your ears. This makes a larger flap to catch sounds. What happens to the sounds you hear?

After your ears catch sound, it travels into the hole in your ear. Then the sound hits a thin piece of skin called the eardrum. The eardrum **vibrates**, and this vibration is passed on to the tiny bones inside your ear.

Right inside your ear there are special hairs. These hairs pick up the movements of the tiny bones and turn them into an electrical **signal**. This signal goes to your brain to tell you that you have heard a sound.

If you listen to lots of loud sounds, these hairs can get damaged. If the hairs stop working, you cannot hear very well.

Your ear collects sound. Your brain turns these vibrations into messages.

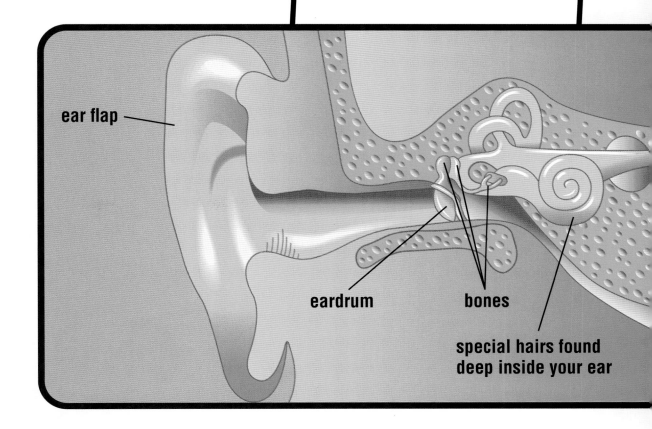

ear flap

eardrum

bones

special hairs found deep inside your ear

How Do We Speak?

Inside your throat there are folds of skin called **vocal chords**. When you speak, you push air from your **lungs** over these. As the air moves over the vocal chords, it makes them **vibrate**. These vibrations make the sound of your voice.

Sound in your life!

Blow up a balloon and hold it by the neck. Now stretch the neck of the balloon out so the air has to push between the bits of rubber in the neck of the balloon. Can you make a sound? This is what you are doing inside your throat when you speak!

The air coming out makes the rubber of the balloon vibrate. This makes a loud squeaking noise.

You use your teeth, lips, and mouth to make different sounds with the vibrations. Say "aahh," "oooo," and "eeee" with your fingers touching your lips. Can you feel the different shapes you make?

Try making different sounds with your teeth, lips, and mouth.

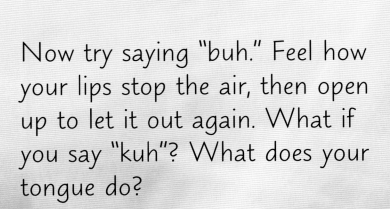

Now try saying "buh." Feel how your lips stop the air, then open up to let it out again. What if you say "kuh"? What does your tongue do?

Animals and Sounds

Animals do not talk, but they can use sounds to send messages. They can send messages to tell another animal about danger, or to scare away an animal that might hurt them.

Cats sometimes hiss at other cats to scare them away. A dog might bark if it wants to go for a walk, or if it hears a strange noise. Even animals in the sea make sounds. Whales make musical sounds that can travel very far to reach other whales in the sea.

This frog makes very loud sounds using the pouch of skin under its mouth.

This bat can use sounds and echoes to find things to eat in the dark.

Some animals can hear sounds that humans cannot hear. A dog can hear very high-pitched sounds that we cannot hear. Some dogs are trained using dog whistles. We cannot hear the whistle sounds, but they are very loud to the dog.

Other animals use sounds and **echoes** to find their way around when they cannot see. Bats send out high-pitched sounds, and then pick up the echo as it bounces off things. This tells them where things are. They can even find tiny insects to eat by picking up these echoes.

Danger!

Sound can be a very useful warning because you can hear it wherever it is coming from. When light is used as a warning, it may get blocked if something is in the way. This does not happen with sound.

When you are crossing the road there is sometimes a light and a sound that helps you know when it is safe to cross. When you hear the sound you know it is safe to cross the road. You should always look and listen before you start crossing!

Sound and light help us to be safe when we cross some roads.

Sound in your life!

How many different kinds of warning sounds can you think of?

A smoke alarm makes a noise if it **detects** smoke. This can save your life because the sound wakes you up if you are asleep.

Sometimes people need to get through traffic very quickly when they are on their way to help someone. Fire engines, police cars, and ambulances have loud sirens so that people can move their cars out of the way and let them through.

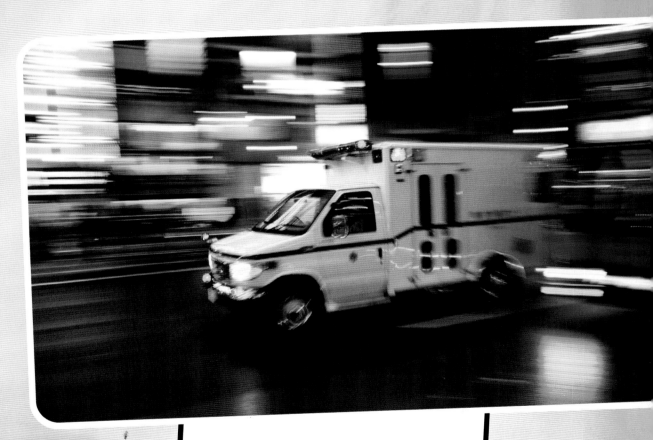

Sound can be used to help clear the way for ambulances.

Sounds in Your Body

Our bodies make lots of noises. Some sounds are made as food passes through your **digestive system**. When food reaches your stomach, **chemicals** break down the food into liquid. This can make gurgling noises. When the food gets further along your digestve system, it can make gas. This can make you burp because your body wants to get rid of the gas.

Doctors can listen to the sounds of your body to find out if you are healthy or not.

Sound in your life!

Put your ear against a friend's stomach and listen to all the gurgles and rumbles as food is digested!

Other moving parts in your body also make sounds. If you are very quiet, you can even hear your heart beating!

Some machines make a very high-pitched sound that we cannot hear. This is called **ultrasound**. By sending ultrasounds into the body and measuring the **echoes**, doctors can make a picture of what is inside. These machines are used to look at babies inside their mothers before they are born!

This machine uses sound and echoes to make a picture of the baby inside this mother's body.

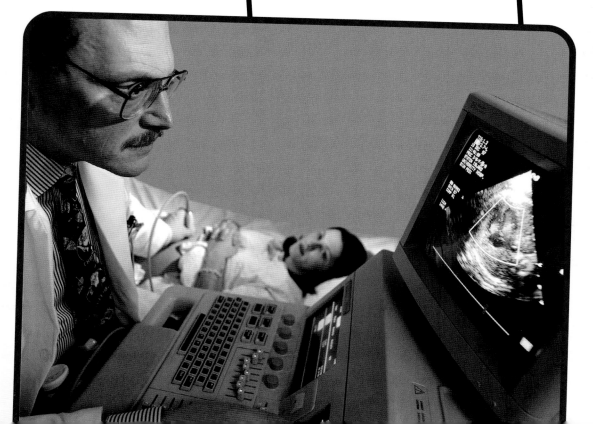

Facts About Sound

Humans can hear a range of sounds from 20 **vibrations** per second up to 20,000 vibrations per second.

Sounds that are faster than 20,000 vibrations per second are called **ultrasound**. Sounds that are slower than 20 vibrations per second are called infrasound.

Elephants can hear very slow vibrations of just 4 per second!

The **volume** or loudness of sound is measured in decibels, or dB for short. Here are some examples of different sounds and how loud they are:

- ticking of a watch—20 dB
- alarm clock—80 dB
- lawn mower—95 dB
- jet airplane engine—130 dB

Did you know?

- Sound travels slightly slower on cold days or in high places!
- Your throat makes different shapes to make different sounds.
- Some airplanes can fly faster than the speed of sound.
- A sperm whale makes the loudest sound of any animal on Earth.

Find Out More

You can find out more about science in everyday life by talking to your teacher or parents. Your local library will also have books that can help. You will find the answers to many of your questions in this book. If you want to know more, you can use other books and the Internet.

More books to read

Cooper, Chris. *Science Answers: Sound.* Chicago: Heinemann Library, 2003.

Hunter, Rebecca. *Discovering Science: Sound.* Chicago: Raintree, 2003.

Parker, Steve. *Science Files: Sound.* Chicago: Heinemann Library, 2004.

Using the Internet

Explore the Internet to find out more about sound. Try using a search engine such as www.yahooligans.com or www.internet4kids.com, and type in keywords such as "**percussion**," "**pitch**," and "**ultrasound**."

Glossary

absorb take in. Some objects absorb sound.

chemical kind of substance. Everything around us is made of chemicals.

code way of sending messages using numbers, letters, or shapes

detects reads or picks up a signal or message

digestive system body parts that break down food

digital when sound is stored as numbers

echo sound that bounces off a surface and comes back to your ears

energy power to make things work. You need energy to get up and walk or run around.

expand get bigger

laser beam powerful light of just one color with a very narrow beam

lung part of your body inside your chest that you breathe air into

material something that objects are made from

MP3 type of computer file that stores music

note musical sound that has different numbers of vibrations in a second. Notes can be put together to make music.

percussion sound made by hitting something. A drum is a percussion instrument.

pitch speed of vibrations in a sound. High-pitched sounds have fast vibrations, and low-pitched sounds have slow vibrations.

reflect bounce off

rhythm repeated pattern of sounds or movements

shockwave sudden movement of air

signal sign or message

surface top or outside part of an object

ultrasound sound that is higher than humans can hear

vibration fast motion up and down or backward and forward

vocal chord thin pieces of skin inside your throat that vibrate when you speak

volume how loud or quiet a sound is

Index